THE FASCINATING WORLD OF SNAKES FOR KIDS

Filled with plenty of facts, information, and photos to learn all about snakes!

A wonderful book for the whole Family!

TABLE OF CONTENTS

INTRODUCTION

Snakes are one of the most fascinating creatures on the planet. With their unique anatomy and behaviour, they have captured the imagination of people for centuries. In this book, we will explore the world of snakes and learn some interesting facts and myths about this amazing creature.

Overview of Snakes

Snakes are reptiles and belong to the suborder Serpentes. They can be found across the globe except in some places, such as Iceland and Ireland. Snakes come in a wide range of shapes and sizes, from the tiny worm snake to the massive reticulated python. These creatures are known for their long, slithering bodies and the scales that cover their skin.

Importance of Snakes in the Ecosystem

Snakes play an important role in the ecosystem. They help to control the populations of other animals, such as rodents, by hunting and eating them.

Snakes are also a crucial part of the food chain, serving as food for many other animals, including birds, mammals, and even other snakes. By maintaining the balance in the ecosystem, snakes help to keep the environment healthy and thriving.

In this book, we will delve deeper into the world of snakes and learn some interesting facts and widely believed myths about these amazing creatures. From their types to anatomy and their role in culture and mythology, there is much to discover about these fascinating animals. So, let's begin our journey into the fascinating world of snakes!

TYPES OF SNAKES

CHAPTER I

Types of Snakes

Snakes come in many different shapes and sizes, and they can be found all over the world. Snakes are a diverse group of reptiles and can be divided into two main categories: non-venomous and venomous. This chapter will discuss the different types of snakes found in each category and their key characteristics.

A. Venomous Snakes

Venomous snakes are those that have venom that is harmful to humans. Venomous snakes are found worldwide but are especially abundant in tropical regions. They are classified into different families based on anatomy, venom composition, and behaviour. Some common families of venomous snakes include,

- Elapidae
- Viperidae
- Hydrophiidae

Elapidae:

Elapidae snakes are a group of venomous snakes found worldwide, primarily in tropical and subtropical regions. Elapid snakes are fast-moving and highly venomous, feeding on a variety of prey, including rodents, birds, and reptiles. They are characterized by their long, slender bodies, short heads, and the presence of venom-delivery systems in the form of fangs.

Examples of elapid species include:

- Indian Cobra

- King Cobra

- Banded Krait

- Inland Taipan

- Coastal Taipan

- Black Mamba

- Green Mamba

King Cobra

Viperidae:

Viperidae is a family of venomous snakes that includes some of the most well-known and widely distributed species of venomous snakes. These snakes are characterized by their distinctive triangular-shaped head, large fangs, and strong venom. They are found in a variety of habitats, from deserts to forests, and are widely distributed throughout the world, except for Australia and Antarctica. Despite their reputation as dangerous and aggressive snakes, vipers are generally shy and will only bite if they feel threatened.

Examples of viperid species include:

- Rattlesnake

- Copperhead

- Cottonmouth

- Pit Vipers

- Adders

- Horned Viper

Rattlesnake

Hydrophiidae:

Hydrophiidae, also known as sea snakes, are a family of venomous snakes that have been adapted to live in the marine environment. They are found in tropical and subtropical waters of the Indo-Pacific region, including the Indian Ocean, the western Pacific Ocean, and the coastlines of Southeast Asia and Australia. Sea snakes have specialized adaptations for life in the water, including a paddle-like tail for swimming, reduced limbs, and the ability to hold their breath for extended periods. They are primarily aquatic and only come to land to bask or lay their eggs.

Examples of hydrophile species include:

- Banded Sea Snake

- Yellow-bellied Sea Snake

- Beaked Sea Snake

- Golden Sea Snake

- Annulated Sea Snake

Banded Sea Snake

B. Non-Venomous Snakes

Non-venomous snakes are those that do not have venom that is harmful to humans. These snakes are generally not dangerous to humans and are often kept as pets. Some common families of non-venomous snakes include,

- Colubridae,
- Xenopeltidae
- Boidae

Colubridae:

They are the most diverse and abundant group of snakes. They can be found in various habitats, including forests, deserts, and grasslands, and are generally harmless to humans. Some well-known species of colubrid snakes include the garter snake, the green snake, the king snake, the rat snake, and the corn snake.

Xenopeltidae:

Xenopeltidae snakes, also known as sunbeam snakes, are a group of non-venomous snakes found in Southeast Asia. They are known for their distinctive appearance, with a shiny, iridescent scale pattern and long, slender bodies. They feed primarily on amphibians and reptiles and are generally non-aggressive toward humans.

Boidae:

Boid snakes, also known as boas, are a group of large, non-venomous snakes that are found in the Americas. They are known for their distinctive shape and large size, with some species growing up to 13 feet long. Boid snakes are generally slow-moving and primarily nocturnal, feeding on a variety of prey, including birds, mammals, and reptiles. Some of the most commonly kept species of boid snakes as pets include boa constrictors, anacondas, and pythons.

Python

ANATOMY OF SNAKES

CHAPTER II

Anatomy of Snakes

Snakes have a unique anatomy that sets them apart from other animals. Snakes are vertebrates, meaning they have a backbone, and their backbone is made up of many vertebrae that are attached to ribs. This unique anatomy allows snakes to be flexible and manoeuvre through tight spaces. In this chapter, we will learn about the different parts of a snake's body and how they help it survive in its environment.

The Head

The head of a snake is very important, as it contains the mouth, eyes, nose, and brain. The shape of the head can tell us a lot about a snake, such as whether it is venomous or not. Venomous snakes typically have triangular-shaped heads, while non-venomous snakes have more rounded heads.

The Body

The body of a snake is long and flexible, allowing it to move easily through tight spaces and to contort itself to escape predators or capture prey. The skin of a snake is covered in scales, which protect and help to regulate its body temperature.

The Tail

The tail of a snake is an important part of its anatomy, as it helps the snake to balance and control its direction when it is moving. Some snakes, such as rattlesnakes, have a rattle on the end of their tails that they can use to make a loud warning noise.

The Fangs

The fangs of a venomous snake are its most important tool for capturing prey and defending itself from predators. Venomous snakes have long, retractable fangs to deliver their venom to their prey or a potential attacker.

The Venom

The venom of a snake is a complex mixture of chemicals that can cause injury or death to a victim. Some venoms are used to subdue prey, while others are used for defence. The type of venom a snake produces depends on the species of snake and the purpose for which the venom is used.

The Senses

Snakes have a range of senses that help them to find food, avoid danger, and navigate their environment. Snakes have a highly developed sense of smell and use their tongue to taste and smell their surroundings. They also have a keen sense of sight and can detect movement and changes in light levels. Some species of snakes, such as the pit viper, can even detect infrared radiation, which allows them to sense the body heat of potential prey.

AMAZING FACTS ABOUT SNAKES

CHAPTER III

Amazing Facts about Snakes

Fact# 1

There are over 3,000 species of snakes.

Snakes are one of the most diverse groups of reptiles, varying greatly in size and shape. They range from the tiny Barbados thread snake, which can grow to just 10 centimetres long, to the reticulated python, which can reach lengths of up to 10 meters.

Unlike other reptiles, snakes do not have legs or limbs.

Snakes have long and flexible bodies that enable them to move in diverse environments such as land, water, and trees. They use their muscles and scales to propel themselves forward and grip surfaces. The absence of limbs gives snakes an edge in terms of stealth and ambush, making them skilled predators in various ecosystems worldwide.

Snakes are found on every continent except Antarctica.

Snakes are cold-blooded and rely on external heat sources to regulate their body temperature and maintain their metabolism. However, in Antarctica, there is insufficient sunlight to provide the warmth that reptiles require, and the scarcity of vegetation and other food sources makes it challenging for them to find enough to eat.

There is an island in Brazil that only has snakes.

Ilha da Queimada Grande, located between Brazil and the Atlantic Ocean, is famously known as Snake Island. With an estimated 5 snakes per square meter, the island is home to a dense population of snakes, primarily the critically endangered golden lanceheads. Whether or not you wish to see that for yourself, access to the island is restricted to tourists due to the presence of these venomous snakes.

Snakes can swallow prey much larger than their own head.

Snakes possess an incredible talent for ingesting prey bigger than their head. This is made possible by their specially adapted jaws and flexible bones in the skull. These unique features enable snakes to stretch their mouths wide open and swallow their prey entirely.

Some species of snakes can "see" infrared radiation.

This ability allows them to detect the body heat of potential prey. This highly specialised adaptation helps snakes locate prey more effectively and increase their chances of survival.

Snakes shed their skin 3-6 times a year.

Snakes periodically shed their skin in a process called ecdysis. This helps remove parasites and damaged skin, promoting growth and health.

Some species of snakes have the ability to constrict and suffocate their prey.

They wrap their bodies around their prey and squeeze tightly, effectively cutting off blood flow and causing the prey to suffocate. This method of hunting is highly effective and allows snakes to take down larger prey than they might otherwise be able to.

The black mamba is the world's fastest snake.

The black mamba is the fastest-moving snake and can instantly move between 4.32 and 5.4 meters per second. These lightning-fast movements are facilitated by its long, slender body, powerful muscles, and streamlined shape.

Snakes are oviparous, ovoviviparous, or viviparous, depending on the species.

Oviparous snakes lay eggs, ovoviviparous snakes retain eggs inside the female until they are ready to hatch, and viviparous snakes give birth to live young. This wide range of reproductive strategies allows snakes to adapt to a wide range of environments and to take advantage of different food and habitat resources.

Flying snakes are real.

Some species of snakes are capable of 'flying' through the air for short distances by flattening their bodies and gliding. This allows them to cover large distances quickly and escape predators.

Snakes navigate by using their tongues.

Since most snakes have weak vision and hearing, they must use their tongues to navigate and find prey. Their forked tongues gather pheromones from their environment, sending messages to the Jacobson's Organ and guiding them on the right path.

Some snakes have the ability to retract their fangs.

When not in use, non-venomous snakes like pythons can retract their fangs into the top of their mouth. This unique adaptation allows these snakes to navigate their environment safely and avoid injury to their fangs.

A snake under stress may eat itself.

Excessive heat can trigger the snake's feeding response, and if there is no available prey, the snake may turn to eat its own body. Unfortunately, once a snake begins to consume itself, it will be unable to stop due to its instinct to hold onto its prey, potentially leading to severe blood loss and death.

Snakes are immune to the venom they produce.

Over time, snakes have developed an immunity to the venom produced by members of their own species, which is important because bites often occur during mating and social interactions. However, it is important to note that this immunity does not extend to venom produced by other snake species.

Snakes don't have external ears.

Yes, it is right, but a snake can still hear, thanks to the vibrations carried to its inner ears by its skin, muscles, and bones.

Snakes can continue to bite even after losing their head.

Although it may sound unbelievable, a snake head that has been severed can still bite and deliver venom for up to an hour after being cut off. This is because of the snake's slow metabolic rate, which allows its organs to remain active for a more extended period of time.

Snakes don't have Eyelids.

It's interesting that snakes don't have eyelids, which means they cannot blink. However, they have a transparent scale called the brille that protects their eyes. As a result, their eyes are always open, and they cannot close them to safeguard against dust, dirt, or other foreign particles.

Some cultures believe that snakes are eternal.

Some cultures view snakes as eternal beings because of their ability to shed their skin, which is seen as a symbol of rebirth and renewal. In ancient mythology, snakes were often depicted as immortal creatures with great wisdom and power. Snakes' circular and spiral movements have also been linked to the concept of eternal life.

All snakes are carnivores and feed on smaller animals for their protein needs.

Most snakes feed on smaller animals, including mammals, birds, reptiles, amphibians, fish, and insects. Some species of snakes feed on specific types of prey, such as rodents, while others are more generalist feeders that will eat a wide range of animals. Their prey also depends on the snake's size, with larger snakes feeding on larger prey and smaller snakes feeding on smaller prey.

Two-headed snakes exist.

Two-headed snakes, also known as bicephalic snakes, are a rare genetic mutation that can occur in the wild. Despite being fascinating and curious, they typically face difficulties in survival as they struggle to coordinate movement, hunt, and eat.

Some snake species are capable of asexual reproduction.

It is a unique and fascinating aspect of snake biology, as not many species have the ability to reproduce asexually. This adaptation allows for quick population growth, especially in scarce mates.

A man once got bitten by a snake but experienced no symptoms.

Nepalese farmer Mohammed Salmodin got into an unexpected battle with a cobra. Despite being bitten, Salmodin fought back by biting the cobra and surprisingly suffered no symptoms—a rare and interesting instance of snake bite immunity.

The black mamba used to have a death rate of 100%.

The black mamba is one of the deadliest snakes in the world; in the past, a bite from a black mamba was often considered a death sentence, with a reported fatality rate of 100%.

Snakes at birth have the same amount of venom as adult snakes.

Newborn snakes are born capable of hunting, as their venom is just as potent as an adult snake. Research has shown that an infant snake's venom is as strong as that of a fully grown one.

Certain animal species have developed a resistance to snake venom.

Certain animal species, such as hedgehogs, mongooses, honey badgers, opossums, and secretary birds, have developed immunity to snake venom.

Snakes typically take 3-5 days to digest a meal.

The warmer a snake's body, the more quickly it can digest its prey. For very large snakes, such as the anaconda, digestion can take weeks.

Snakes can weigh up to 250 Kg.

The heaviest snake in the world is the Green Anaconda. It weighs over 550 pounds (250 kg) and can grow to over 30 feet (9m) long. It has been known to eat caimans, capybaras, and jaguars.

Some species of snakes, such as the Anaconda, are excellent swimmers.

Anacondas are known to be among the strongest swimmers of all snakes, capable of propelling themselves through fast-moving rivers and lakes with ease. Additionally, they use the water as a habitat to hunt prey ambush predators and escape danger.

Snakes can survive up to a year without eating.

Snakes can survive for long periods without food, sometimes up to a year without eating. This is due to several adaptations, including slow digestion and the ability to store energy as fat in their bodies. Some species of snakes, such as the python, can go for several months without eating after a large meal, while others, such as the rattlesnake, may only need to eat a few times a year.

Snakes can emit light.

Some snake species, like the banded krait, possess bioluminescent properties and can emit a bright blue light from specific glands on their skin. The exact reason behind this bioluminescence has yet to be well understood. However, some scientists speculate that it might serve the purpose of frightening predators away, attracting potential mates, or signalling to other snakes.

Snakes are good actors.

Some species of snakes, such as the hognose snake, can " play dead" when faced with danger; these snakes will often collapse to the ground, lie still, and even emit a foul smell to convince a predator that they are not worth attacking.

Did you know that snakes can have as many as 200 teeth?

However, these teeth are not used for chewing food but instead are pointed backwards to prevent prey from escaping once consumed.

Snakes are fully protected by keratin scales, even on their eyes.

Snakes are covered in scales from head to tail, including their eyes. These scales serve as protective armour for the snake, helping to keep its skin moist and safeguarded from damage and injury. The scales are made from keratin, the same material that forms human hair.

Snakes use their throats to drink water.

Snakes do not lap up water as mammals do; instead, they dunk their snouts underwater and use their throats to pump water into their stomachs.

Snakes regrow worn-out teeth continuously.

A snake's fangs typically last for 6 to 10 weeks before they start to wear down. When this happens, a new fang begins to grow in its place, ensuring that the snake always has a sharp and functional set of teeth.

In 2014, a man was eaten alive by a 25 ft anaconda.

A conservationist named Paul Rosolie attempted an unprecedented feat – being swallowed by an anaconda and surviving. To ensure his safety, he wore a custom-made carbon fibre suit equipped with a breathing system, cameras, and a communication system. Despite meticulous preparations, the formidable grip of the anaconda proved to be a force beyond anticipation for Rosolie. The power exerted by the snake's constriction became overwhelming, prompting him to abort the daring stunt. Rosolie, fearing that the immense pressure might lead to a fracture in his arm, prioritized his safety and called off the unprecedented interaction with the giant serpent. The scientific community responded to Rosolie's venture with a wave of criticism. Experts expressed concerns about the inherent dangers the stunt posed, not only to Rosolie but also to the well-being of the anaconda. Moreover, the act was condemned for potentially establishing a hazardous precedent for future encounters between humans and wildlife, as it showcased a level of interaction that could jeopardize the safety of both parties involved.

Snakes eat only 6–30 meals each year.

Snakes are known for their low metabolism and ability to survive on minimal food. In fact, snakes typically need to eat only 6 to 30 meals yearly to maintain their health.

Have you ever wondered how snakes can consume prey larger than their own bodies without choking?

Snakes have an interesting solution to avoid the risk of choking. They can push the end of their trachea, or windpipe, out of their mouth, similar to how a snorkel works. This allows them to breathe while they swallow their prey whole without risking choking or suffocation.

Sea snakes can dive up to 300 feet deep into the ocean.

Their paddle-shaped tails provide improved manoeuvrability and hydrodynamic efficiency, enabling them to dive deep into the ocean in search of food or avoid predators.

Snakes can spit venom at distances up to 8 feet.

The Mozambique Spitting Cobra is known for its remarkable ability to spit venom over distances of up to 8 feet. This cobra can spit its venom from any position, whether lying on the ground or raised, making it a formidable opponent.

Unlike other animals, snakes never stop growing throughout their lives.

Although snakes' growth rate slows as they age, they can continue to grow throughout their entire life, sometimes reaching lengths of several meters.

Snake soup has been a popular dish in Cantonese cuisine for over 2,000 years.

This flavorful soup was made from a variety of ingredients, including snake meat, herbs, and spices, and is said to have many health benefits. So, the next time you hear someone talking about snake soup, remember that it's much more than just a bowl of soup - it's a culinary tradition that has been enjoyed for centuries.

Would you dare to drink snake blood?

In some Asian countries, there is a belief that consuming the blood of a snake, specifically the cobra, can increase sexual virility. This belief has led to a dangerous practice where the blood is drained from a live cobra and then mixed with liquor.

Snakes can live from 4 to over 25 years.

It is interesting to observe the differences in lifespans among different species of snakes. For instance, the garter snake, known for having a relatively shorter lifespan, manages to make the most out of its existence within 4 to 6 years. On the other hand, the king cobra, a majestic serpent, is known for its longevity, thriving for over 25 years.

Snake teeth are always curved backwards.

Unlike humans, snakes don't chew with their teeth. Instead, their curved teeth are used to keep prey from escaping the snake's mouth.

A multi-faceted symbol throughout history.

The snake has been a symbol in various cultures and religions throughout history, and its interpretations have been multi-faceted. For instance, in ancient Egyptian mythology, the snake was associated with royalty and divine authority. In Hinduism, the snake is a symbol of Kundalini, the divine energy that lies dormant within every human being. Similarly, in ancient Greek mythology, the snake was associated with healing and medicine and with the god of medicine, Asclepius. In other cultures, however, the snake has been interpreted negatively. In the Bible, the snake is portrayed as the embodiment of evil, tempting Eve to eat the forbidden fruit and thus bringing about the downfall of humanity. In some African cultures, the snake is associated with witchcraft and black magic. Overall, the snake has been a symbol of positive and negative qualities throughout history, reflecting the complexity of human beliefs and values.

Did you know that in addition to slithering on the ground, some snakes can glide through the air?

That's right! There are five species of flying snakes that have been observed gliding through the trees of Southeast Asia and soaring up to 330 feet (100 meters) in the air. These amazing creatures have specially adapted flat bodies, small scales, and the ability to control their movements through the air, making them true airborne marvels!

Fact# 49

Get ready to be amazed! Meet the Arafura snake - a species that's so rare and unique!

It only lays a single egg once every decade! These snakes are
pretty conservationists, conserving their energy by eating less often. Despite eating less often, the Arafura snake can survive and thrive in its environment.

Fact# 50

Snakes have a diverse reproductive system.

While the majority of snakes lay eggs, those living in colder climates have adapted to give live birth, eliminating the need to lay eggs in unfavourable conditions.

The fastest snake can travel up to 12 miles per hour.

The black mamba is one of the fastest snakes in the world; with its long, slender body and lightning-fast speed, this serpent can slither along at a shocking pace of up to 12 miles per hour! Whether chasing down prey or escaping from danger, the black mamba is a formidable force to be reckoned with.

Snakes have a long evolutionary history, believed to date back to 142 million years ago.

While it is difficult to determine the exact date of their evolution, evidence of snakes first appearing in the fossil record dates back to the Cretaceous period. Scientists believe their first appearance in the fossil record puts their age anywhere between 98 and 142 million years, making them younger than other reptiles such as crocodiles, lizards, and turtles.

Snakes are more active during the night.

Snakes are nocturnal animals, meaning they are most active during the night. Unlike other animals that use their vision as the primary sense to locate prey or avoid danger, snakes rely heavily on their sense of smell to hunt and detect potential threats. When visibility is limited at night, their sense of smell becomes more acute, allowing them to hunt for food or avoid danger effectively.

Baby snakes typically start hunting for food immediately after hatching or being born.

Baby snakes typically undergo a remarkable phase lasting about a week, during which they do not require nourishment. However, once they reach readiness, their inherent hunting instinct comes to the forefront. Despite their tender age, these young serpents exhibit impressive skills in hunting and capturing prey, showcasing the early development of their predatory abilities.

Some species of snakes live in the ocean, known as sea snakes.

Sea snakes are a group of species that have evolved to live in the ocean. They have adapted to the marine environment and possess unique features such as flattened tails that aid in swimming and nostril valves that enable them to breathe while submerged. These remarkable reptiles highlight these creatures' extraordinary range of adaptation, as they can thrive in the open ocean's challenging and constantly changing conditions.

Did you know snakes are defensive, not aggressive animals?

Snakes are not naturally aggressive animals and tend to avoid human interactions. They do not actively seek out conflict or bite humans out of malice. Instead, they prefer to remain hidden and avoid any encounters.

Snakes are bony – they can have up to 1,200 bones.

Snakes are vertebrates, meaning they have a backbone, and their backbones comprise many vertebrae attached to ribs. Unlike humans, who have 24 ribs, a total of 206 bones, snakes can have up to 33 ribs, giving them up to 1200 bones.

All snakes are born swimmers.

Snakes are naturally skilled swimmers and can swim from a very young age. They swim by making lateral, wavelike movements that start at the head and continue down to the tail.

Snake's heart is capable of moving within its body.

Snakes are known for their incredible adaptations, and one of the most remarkable is the ability of their heart to move within their body. This unique adaptation allows the heart to shift its position to protect itself when a large prey item is passing through the oesophagus. As the snake consumes its meal, the heart can move and defend itself from being compressed or damaged by the passing prey.

The fear of snakes is called philophobia or herpetophobia.

Philophobia refers to a general fear of snakes, while herpetophobia refers explicitly to a fear of reptiles, including snakes. This fear is a common phobia and affects many people around the world. It can range from mild anxiety to severe and debilitating fear and can impact an individual's daily life.

Snake bites cause up to 138,000 deaths annually.

It is estimated that up to 2.7 million people are bitten by snakes each year, resulting in up to 138,000 deaths. Most of these deaths occur in Africa and South Asia, where venomous snake species are prevalent, and antivenom treatment is not widely available.

Snake venom is currently being studied for its potential use in cancer treatment.

The study of snake venom and its potential medical applications is an area of ongoing research. One of the properties of many snake venoms is the ability to kill cells, known as the cytotoxic effect. The idea is that the cytotoxic effect of the venom could be harnessed to target and destroy cancer cells while leaving healthy cells unscathed.

The study of snakes is called Ophiology.

Ophiology is the scientific study of snakes, including their anatomy, physiology, behaviour, and evolutionary history. Ophiology is a subfield of herpetology which studies reptiles and amphibians.

Did you know that venom and poison are often considered the same?

While English distinguishes between venom and poison, many languages use a single word to describe both. Venom is something injected, and the poison is something ingested. There are snakes in the world with both venomous and poisonous defence mechanisms.

Snakes can also move in a straight line.

Going beyond the common S-shaped slither, snakes have the remarkable ability to move in a straight line using rectilinear locomotion. This stealthy technique is mainly used by heavy-bodied snakes while hunting their prey.

Sea snakes can't breathe underwater.

Contrary to popular belief, sea snakes cannot breathe underwater and must surface for air. Most snakes can 'breathe' through their skin and have a large lung encompassing almost half their length to retain oxygen.

Did you know that even small and seemingly defenceless snakes can use their voice as a powerful weapon of defence?

Their hissing sound, created by forcing air through their glottis in the throat, is a way for them to warn and intimidate potential predators. So, the next time you encounter a hissing snake, remember it's using its voice to protect itself.

Snakes can steal heat.

Surprised! That's correct. Some snakes, especially garter snakes, employ a unique way of regulating their body temperature called kleptothermy. They do so by approaching another snake and absorbing its heat, making the victim snake colder as warmth is transferred. This behaviour is not reciprocal, meaning the heat-stealing snake benefits while the victim does not.

Did you know that snake venom can be quite expensive?

The value of snake venom can range from $50 to $5,000 per gram, depending on the type of snake and the demand for that particular type of venom.

Have you ever considered having a snake as a pet? Yes, you can. Snakes are good pets.

Although not as popular as cats, dogs, or rabbits, snakes are kept as pets by many people worldwide. Over a million people are estimated to own at least one snake in their homes. While they may not be affectionate or cuddly, they are fascinating and require less maintenance than other pets. Unlike dogs, they don't need daily exercise; some species only need to be fed once a week or two. Though they may not suit everyone, snakes can make good pets due to their low maintenance and intriguing nature.

MYTHS ABOUT SNAKES

CHAPTER IV

Myths About Snakes

For centuries, snakes have been surrounded by myths and superstitions, leading to many misconceptions and baseless beliefs about these reptiles. Among these myths is the idea that snakes can control the weather, influence luck, or have mystical powers. These unrealistic notions have created a complex narrative around snakes, attributing qualities beyond reality to them. In folklore, snakes are frequently portrayed as symbolic figures associated with danger, malice, and cunning. The stories often depict these creatures as enemies, creating an atmosphere of fear and distrust towards these fascinating animals. The elaborate tapestry of folklore has contributed to a long-standing cultural perception that sometimes misrepresents snakes' true nature and hides their ecological role in various ecosystems. In this chapter, we will explore some of the most widely believed myths about snakes.

Myth # 1

"snakes are deaf"

For many years, scientists believed that snakes could not hear due to the absence of visible ears and their tendency to not respond to sound. This led to the common misconception that snakes were deaf. However, recent research has revealed that snakes can detect vibrations and recognize sounds in a unique way. They are equipped with specialized sensory structures, such as the Jacobson's organ in their mouths, which allows them to detect vibrations in the ground and recognize sounds in their environment. Additionally, snakes have sensitive skin that can detect changes in air pressure, allowing them to pick up on the vibrations created by sound waves. This means snakes can detect and respond to sounds despite their lack of visible ears. These findings have revolutionized our understanding of snake sensory capabilities and have debunked the myth that snakes are deaf.

Myth # 2

"where baby snakes are, mothers follow"

The saying "where baby snakes are, mothers follow" is a common misconception about the behaviour of snake mothers. Unlike many other animals, such as bears, snakes do not exhibit strong maternal instincts and do not protect their young. In the wild, mother snakes do not stay with their babies after they are born or hatched. Instead, they leave them on their own to hunt and feed for themselves. Baby snakes are equipped with their own hunting instincts, which allows them to survive and find food without the protection of their mother. This behaviour reflects snakes' survival strategy, as mothers are often unable to provide long-term care for their young in the wild. Instead, they focus on their survival and reproduction, leaving their offspring to defend themselves.

Myth # 3

"venom should be sucked out"

The myth that venom should be sucked out after a snake bite is a common belief that has been perpetuated by Hollywood movies. However, this method of treating a snake bite is ineffective and can worsen the situation. Venom spreads quickly through the bloodstream and can cause severe damage to the body. Sucking the venom out or cutting the affected area will not stop the spread of venom and can even introduce bacteria into the wound, increasing the risk of infection. The most effective way to treat a snake bite is to seek immediate medical attention and receive an anti-venom injection as soon as possible. This will help to neutralize the venom and prevent further damage to the body. It is important to remember that snake bites can be life-threatening and require prompt and proper medical treatment.

Myth # 4

"Snakes are boneless"

The myth that snakes are boneless is a common misconception. Snakes, like all other vertebrates, do, in fact, have bones. However, their bones are much smaller and more flexible than human bones, which gives them their characteristic fluid movements and contortions. The skeleton of a snake comprises hundreds of small, individual bones connected by flexible joints, allowing them to move and twist in ways that would be impossible for other animals with larger, more rigid bones. Despite their small size, snake bones play an important role in supporting their bodies, protecting their vital organs, and allowing them to move and hunt effectively. So, while snakes may appear boneless to the untrained eye, they are, in fact very much filled with bones.

Myth # 5

"Snakes are slimy"

The myth that snakes are slimy is often perpetuated in popular culture. However, this is far from true. Snakes do not secrete mucus or other slippery substances, and they are quite dry to the touch. In fact, many species of snakes are adapted to live in desert environments, where water is scarce, and they cannot produce sweat to regulate their body temperature. Instead, they rely on behaviours like basking in the sun, burrowing into the ground, or retreating into shady crevices to regulate their temperature. So, while snakes may appear slimy because of the smooth, slippery texture of their scales, they are, in fact, dry and do not secrete any substances that would make them slippery to the touch. By learning the truth about snakes and dispelling common misconceptions, we can appreciate these remarkable animals for their valuable contributions to our world.

CONCLUSION

CHAPTER V

Conclusion

In this chapter, we will recap the key points covered in the previous chapters and provide some final thoughts on snakes.

A. Recap of Key Points

Throughout the book, we explored their anatomy, unravelling the mysteries that make these creatures unique. From the mesmerizing behaviours that define their existence to the diverse habitats they call home, our journey has uncovered the tapestry of their lives. Feasting upon the knowledge surrounding their diets, we've learned about the remarkable adaptations that enable snakes to thrive in various ecosystems. Alongside these insights, we've ventured into the captivating realm of interesting facts, unearthing nuggets of information that paint a vivid portrait of the astonishing diversity within the snake kingdom.

We've navigated the realm of myths that have enveloped these creatures for centuries, exploring the often misunderstood narratives surrounding them. Through the annals of history, we've uncovered snakes' complex relationship with humanity, weaving a narrative that intertwines with culture and mythology.

B. Final Thoughts on Snakes

Snakes are fascinating creatures that play important roles in the ecosystem and have a rich cultural history. While they can sometimes be seen as dangerous or frightening, it is important to remember that most snakes are not aggressive and will only bite if they feel threatened. By learning about snakes and their behaviour, we can better understand these amazing animals and appreciate their important roles in our world.

We hope that this book has provided a comprehensive introduction and interesting facts about snakes for kids, and we encourage you to continue learning about these fascinating creatures. Whether you encounter a snake in the wild or in a zoo, take some time to observe and appreciate these unique and important animals.

Five Tips to Avoid Snake Bites

When hiking, remain on the designated trail for easier visibility and to minimize the chance of encountering a snake.

Wear protective gear, such as boots and long pants, when entering snake-populated areas as most snakes are found on the ground and may target feet and legs.

Be alert and cautious when in snake territory. Snakes may hide and remain still while waiting for prey, so inspect your surroundings before sitting on logs, handling rocks, or gathering firewood.

Avoid approaching snakes. A seemingly lifeless snake may actually be a dormant one ready to strike, so keep a safe distance and retreat slowly instead of risking an encounter.

If a snake enters your home, do not try to capture it yourself. Instead, exit the premises and contact local animal control for safe removal.

Thank you for choosing and trusting us!

Don't forget to share your experience and give a review on Amazon.

US

UK

Made in the USA
Las Vegas, NV
12 September 2024

95165257R00046